ON LYCANTHROPY, TRANSFORMATION & ECSTASY OF SORCERERS

Edited by KAZIm

Foreword by VINI DE MONTE

English translation by MARINA RIVAS GARCÍA

*

Cover woodcut by Michael Wolgemut (1434-1519)
from the Nuremberg Chronicle

Fist page : 'Satyr' by Edvard Munch (1908)

Additional illustration by Bernard Zuber

*

Original title : DE LA LYCANTHROPIE,
TRANSFORMATION ET EXTASE DES SORCIERS

First published in Paris (1615)

English translation realised after the Spanish translation
made by Marina Rivas García & published by Ediciones Nyktelios

No part of this publication may be reproduced or transmitted in any form or by any means, electronic or mechanical, including photocopy or any storage and retrieval system, without permission in writing from the publisher.

ISBN : 978-2-492143-12-0

© HEXEN PRESS

ON LYCANTHROPY,
Transformation &
Ecstasy of Sorcerers.

Wherein the Devil's trickery is put to the test, such that it is henceforth impossible, even for the most ignorant, to be seduced thereby.

Including a refutation of the arguments that Bodin alleges in chapter six of the second book of his *Demonomania*, in favor of the supposed transformation of men into beasts.

The whole composed by J. DE NYNAULD,

Doctor of Medicine.

PARIS - MDCXV

.: FOREWORD :.
by *Vini de Monte*

The publication of *De La Lycanthropie* marked a significant shift in the understanding of lycanthropy and its association with witchcraft. At the dawn of the 17th century, within the Catholic Church, the representation of witchcraft as a real act in itself, as well as the processes of theriomorphosis, were subject to debate. Much of the ecclesiastical sector remained clinging to what the *Canon Episcopi* ruled about the illusions of night flights and encounters with the Devil. However, the common people and a small faction within the Church kept believing in the veracity of these facts. In the Kingdoms of Spain, witchcraft as a heretical act was hardly persecuted. Its greatest exposure was in the northern kingdoms (Navarra, Galicia, lordship of Vizcaya), especially during the one hundred and fifty years after the Papal Bull of Innocent VIII (1484), entitled *"Summis desiderantis affectibus"* and the writing of the *Malleus Maleficarum* (1486), where witchcraft not only becomes a crime against faith, but where all its manifestations become real.

The vision of the diabolical witch, as depicted in the numerous works that supported the belief in their existence, primarily originated from the Kingdom of France. Its detractors were usually notable figures, such as ecclesiastics and graduates, like the author of this work, Jean de Nynauld. Within this controversial debate, the content of this book somewhat created a schism in favor of more rationalist positions regarding witchcraft and the belief in witches transforming into animals such as wolves and dogs. Jean de Nynauld, drawing from his medical knowledge, contributed an empirical view in which he largely acknowledged a physiological alteration as a trigger for lycanthropy, without disregarding the participation of those elements that cloud the mind: *the poisons*.

The poisons shown in the treatise are organized by the author by the supposed effects they have on the psyche, thus constructing a categorization of the famous witches' ointment. The identification of botanical and animal species was carried out through the analysis of other medical texts. For this, historical references have been used, renowned treatises on Materia Medica and local antidote books, such as the translation of *De Materia Medica* by Doctor Andrés Laguna (1555), *Liber Simplicis Medicinae* by Hidelgarda de Bingen (1143) among others.

In addition to the pharmacological systematization, this in turn responds to the thesis of another illustrious person of the time, Jean Bodin, one of the greatest exponents of Positive Demonology in the Kingdom of France. One of the highlights of de Nynauld's work is the critical examination of Bodin's theories as presented in his renowned treatise *De la Démonomanie des Sorciers* (1580). This theological debate ultimately favored rationalist and materialist perspectives. By the middle of the 17th century, the belief in witchcraft as a reality gradually diminished in Europe, particularly within the Inquisition. In the Kingdom of Granada (Spain), a 1615 inquisitorial report to Margaret of Naples, accused of "casting lots" with beans, acknowledged that this practice was not deemed heretical or sinful, since all women carried it out and considered it a mere household game. In 1625, the Superior Council of the Inquisition convened in the same city to deliberate on the reality of witches' heretical practices, resulting in 6 'Yes' and 4 'No' votes. Although this seemed perhaps like a lost battle for rationalist positions, the Inquisition never enforced such persecution into practice in Spain, contrary to common belief.

The search for a rational understanding of magic, night flights and raising the dead from more rationalist positions made the philosophers of the time turn to popular beliefs to expose what they considered an act of ignorance. Paradoxically, without realizing it, those who wanted to condemn heretical beliefs left in their handwriting a very valuable testimony of folklore and popular visions about beings of the night, witches and their diabolical synagogues, as well as the nature of the soul, and its ability to temporarily leave the body and to interact in the physical world from the other side. Likewise, De Nynauld's only fully preserved treatise contains a wealth of valuable information about the ecstatic experiences of witches and the phenomenon of the ointments. We cannot interpret this information in any other way than an analysis from a proto-ethnopharmacological perspective of the social phenomenon. In *De la Lycanthropie*, the interpretation of the properties of plants is very detailed in comparison to what was known at the time about their effectiveness as disruptive agents of reason. It is without a doubt the first work that explains in detail the physiological properties of the substances that made up the different witches' ointments. Furthermore, it describes how these ointments managed to provoke, upon exposure to the drug, various classic manifestations of flight such as drowsiness, agitated madness (delirium tremens), visions, etc.

The translation of Jean de Nynauld's original work, first into Spanish and now into English, represents a global advancement in understanding the phenomenon of witchcraft, its history and related mysticism. And, through deep reading, one can dive into the great mysteries and knowledge that the folklore and beliefs of our ancestors carried with them.

BOTANICAL & ANIMAL IDENTIFICATION TABLE:

Translation	Original text	Species
Hoopoe (blood)	Huppe	Upupa epops
Aconite	Aconit	Aconitum napellus
Poplar (leaves)	Peuplier	Populus spp.
Aloe (wood)	Áloes	Species of Aquilaria genre
Poppies	Pavour	Species of Papaver genre, different to P. somniferum. Possibly P. rhoeas
Anachitides	Anachitides	Unknown

Celery	Ache	Species of the genres: Apium (Apium graveolens), Helosciadium (H. nordiflorum; H. inundatum; H. repens).
Black henbane	Hyosciame	Species of the Hyosciamus genre, possibly H. niger o H. albus.
Deadly nightshade	Belladona	Atropa belladonna
Lesser water-parsnip/ cutleaf waterparsnip/ narrow-leaved water-parsnip	Berla	Berula erecta
Heather	Bruyere	Erica spp
Sweet flag/ sway/ muskrat root	Acorum Vulgaire	Acorus calamus
Hemlock	Cyguë	Cicuta virosa; Conium maculatum
Hedgehog	Herisson	Erinaceus europeaus
Datura stramonium	Stramonium	Datura stramonium
Cat	Chat	Felis silvestris catus
Centípede	Geotephillide	Chilopoda
Cannabis	Heiranluc	Cannabis indica
Ashwagandha	Morelle Endormante	Withania somnífera

Deadly nightshade	Morelle Furieuse	Atropa belladona; Solanum nigrum
Soot	Suye	Does not apply
Wolf	Loup	Canis lupus
Mint	Mente	Mentha spp.
Myrrh	Myrrhe	Commiphora myrrha
Bat (blood)	Chauve	Species of the quirópteros genre
Opium	Opium	Papaver somniferum
Palm of Christ	Palme Christi	Ricinus communis
Peony	Piuoine	Paenonia spp
Parsley	Persil	Petroselinum crispum
Cinquefoils/ Five fingers/ Silverweeds	Pentaphilon	Potentilla spp.
Roses	Roses	Rosa spp.
Toad	Crapaud	Bufo bufo
Snake	Serpent	Vipera Verus
Datura stramonium	Solanum	Datura stramonium
Synochytides	Synochytides	Unknown
Thyme	Thymia	Thymus vulgaris
Violets	Violettes	Viola odorata
Plantains/ Fleaworts	Psellium	Plantago psyllium
Fox	Renard	Vulpes vulpes

TO MY LORD,
THE ILLUSTRIOUS & REVEREND
JACQUES DU PERRON, CARDINAL,

Grand Parish Priest of France, Archbishop of Sens, Primate of Gaul & Germania.

My LORD,

Among all the things that seem worthy of great astonishment to the common people, lycanthropy & the abduction of the soul out of the body, easily occupy the first place. The more it surpasses the senses, the more admirable it is to men.

That is why the common people cannot understand & learn the causes of a real transformation, & yet, this appearance or transformation confirmed by the confession of Sorcerers is deferred to the Demons. Very impious opinion, which I intend to refute by this little treaty to maintain the glory of God against the wiles of the Devil, & to deprive people from sinning through ignorance.

Now, as much as envy & slander usually attack those who undertake something great, I turn to you, My Lord, to be a safe refuge for me against those who would contradict me.

The truth that I hold & the glory of God which I maintain give me the assurance that you overshadow with your favor this modest writing of mine which cannot meet entirely the merit of the subject. Do better whoever can, & in a higher style. As far as I am concerned, I shall be satisfied that you approve it & feel sufficiently rewarded if you will deign to support me.

My LORD,

Your humble & obedient servant
JEAN DE NYNAULD.

ON LYCANTHROPY,
TRANSFORMATION &
ECSTASY OF SORCERERS.

That men cannot, by any means of the Devil, be transformed into beasts, the same that the Devil cannot separate the soul from the body of Sorcerers, so that after some time it returns to their body.

.: CHAPTER ONE :.

HOW MUCH the Devil, to gain the credit over humans, by turning them from God, acts as a malicious monkey to counterfeit the admirable works of our God. The Devil can in no way change the essences of things than by illusion, an illusion however, that can only be understood correctly by those who are slaves to him, & sometimes, with divine permission, due to unbelievers of the Christian faith.

Therefore, Sorcerers say in their confessions that they have been transformed into crows, magpies, wolves, boars, cats, mice, serpents & other similar animals, & that being in the form of a raven they have flown & croaked, & in the shape of a serpent, they crawled, & in the form of a cat they have entered through small spaces, in the proportions of the body of a real cat. Likewise, in the form of a wolf, they stalk the countryside, devouring infants, killing sheep & other similar things, all after anointing the body with certain ointments that the Devil gave them to use.

This is only a fable, a pure illusion of the Devil, who deceives the senses of his slaves who have taken refuge in him, & those who believe in such things are unworthy of the Christian name & contempt by God, since they depart from His Glory & they attribute to Him powers similar to those of the Devil, sworn enemy of God, Creator of the Universe & the human race. For this reason, they falsely attribute to the Devil the power of changing the essence of things. This power only belongs to one God, of whom he is jealous of his glory as I shall show below.

Therefore, in order to divert the infidels of the Christian faith from such impious credulities, I will expound the cause of these things & show how they are & their purposes, beginning first with the metamorphosis of men into beasts, in which Bodin in chapter 6 of the second book of his *Demonomania* confirms & assures that this is real. This is not real, it is against right, reason, & against theological & philosophical maxims.

I say against theological maxims since it is blasphemy to say & believe that the Devil can really change the nature of things against the natural ability that the Creator gives to them. If that was the case, we would have to establish two principles, which is another blasphemy. We must not, therefore, consider that God wants to communicate to the evil spirits (whom he deprived of his grace & assigned to eternal fire) the power to create or change the essence of things, since this power is reserved to God alone & that is why, according to the Bible, he is called par excellence, the Creator. Our Lord Jesus Christ makes mention of this power when he says that "God is able to raise up children to Abraham from the stones". These things along with a million others are impossible to attribute to the Devil, according to the Bible & the common consent of Theologians.

The Devil cannot give the slightest virtue or property to anything at all, much less can he create anything out of nothing. Nor could he transmute a body into salt, as God transformed Lot's wife. He cannot truly transmute rods into Serpents, nor water into blood, nor beget frogs, nor transform the dust of the earth into lice. Nor can he split the sea to pass through the waves, nor give sweetness to salt water, nor make it come out of contact with stone. All those things, however, have been accomplished by Moses.

The Devil cannot enlarge small things as we often see happening to seeds & other things created by God. He cannot restore sight to Angels, raise the dead or change water into wine & he cannot give life to things, as our Lord Jesus Christ did. The Devil cannot make iron float, as Elisha did. Nor can he prevent, corrupt or reverse the divinely instituted natural course, as Joshua did, fighting against the Amorites, & Isaiah when he assured King Hezekiah that he would be restored to health, & Jesus

Christ when he hung on the Cross. He also could not restore destroyed things, nor make the Moon descend from Heaven, or love good people & hate the wicked, or to know the secret thoughts of the heart. The Devil cannot do any of those things without the permission of our Lord Jesus Christ, much less could he enter the bodies of men at the will, imprecation or curse of any Sorcerer. Finally, the Devil cannot foresee or guess how God wills to dispose of his creatures or His empires before the proper God spoke by His mouth.

As this alleged transformation on the part of Witches is repugnant to the highest Theologians, it is also repugnant to the highest Philosophers, since Philosophers believed & held a common agreement that one species cannot be transformed into a different species. Likewise, that a perfect form cannot become a rough & coarse matter. For this reason, Aristotle says that every body is made for its form & according to its perfection, & not the other way around, according to which the body is an instrument of the form. Then, how is it that by the virtue of an ointment, or other means of the Devil, the body of a Sorcerer can be transformed into a wolf, or into other animals? This is not possible because it has been shown metaphysically that this can only be done by the Creator of the Universe, since some forms cannot be transformed into other different forms.

If it was true what the Sorcerers claimed, the bodily form of man would have to change into that of a wolf, the form of the human body would perish & after that the form of a wolf would arise in matter (which cannot be possible as I have already shown). This is false, because if it were so, when the form of the human body perishes, the soul would separate from the body & go to the place that God has ordained & would never return. Now, the soul cannot be separated from the body unless it has first been deprived of all of its three natural faculties, which are Vital, Animal, & Natural faculties. If these perish, death follows, the soul is separated from the body &, being free, returns to its original source from which it will not take shape again until the resurrection of the dead, as every true Christian believes.

Now, we will see if from the matter of this body a wolf can be made. First of all, this is repugnant to any order of nature, since nature cannot generate nor form such an animated body by a subject which is not animated by a certain power, as the Philosophers say, because everything that brings into being, or is born, comes from seed, or is seedless, & is Vegetative or Animal. So, that which is vegetative multiplies & is born out of the seed of its species. The seed, then, is sown, either by itself or by others at the proper time. That which has no seed multiplies by its roots or branches cut off & planted in a reasonable time so that the species may not perish, & it is done by the providence of God.

As for Animals, they are either perfect or imperfect. Perfect Animals can engender nothing but by the sperm of the male in conjunction with the female in copulation of the same species. Then, there is nothing like this supposed & fantastic metamorphosis, therefore I conclude that this is only a pure fable & illusion of the Devil. But let us see how one absurdity is followed by several absurdities.

Therefore, it should be noted that, having believed in this transformation of men into beasts, it is asserted & believed that Sorcerers can change into the forms of cats, crows, or serpents, & that they can enter through those holes or folding doors, which are only the size of the form they believe they have taken. To believe in all these impostures is a ridiculous & monstrous thing to which no answer is deserved, since such a thing is as impossible to the Devil, as it is to him also to make a camel pass through the hole of a pin, which our Savior God always considered an impossible thing. Because the body & all that is included in it have a capacity, so that whatever is lodged in it must be proportioned to that place. Otherwise, it would be necessary to warn that there would be penetration of bodies, which is against nature & any principle of physics.

Here someone may object that the body transformed into a cat can only have the size of a natural cat, & that therefore it can enter through the openings of its size. But to this affirmation I reply that the solid human body which is composed of bones, nerves, arteries, tendons, muscles, flesh, membranes & skin cannot be reduced to a body as small as a cat. This is because no body can be annulled, nor can it be created or transformed in any way, but only by the one God, author & custodian of all things that are to be.

As for the fact that our Lord Jesus Christ went to see his disciples & passed to the room when the doors were closed because of their fear of the Jews, this does not mean that the Sorcerers through the Devil can do the same. For who would be so impious & cruel as to want to equal or compare the power of the Devil (which he has only borrowed) with the omnipotence of Jesus Christ? For the Devil will not be able to do any of the things we have said above, least of all that the same body would be at the same time in several places, & even less that a witch would go to the Synagogue only in spirit & return having separated herself from the body.

Let us now continue the thread of our discourse & bring to light the artifice & tricks of this Old Serpent, enemy of God & of Mankind who, due to his prideful wish to equal our God, was thrown into Hell & forever deprived of His Grace. His pride, therefore, which was the first cause of his punishment, is also the cause of all these illusions & impostures, because desperate to ever return to Grace, he turned himself against the Eternal & tried to seduce & turn men away from the fervor they owe to God, to draw them to him & to have companions (which is the only consolation of the miserable). Or better still, he attempts to counterfeit the works of God, obscuring & diminishing, if possible, His glory & power & consequently attributing things to himself by means of false miracles & illusions.

Thus, he thought he was admirable & made himself worshipped, prayed to, & honored by ignorant heathens, barbarians, & infidels who prevaricated. He is not content with having seduced them once & win, but he promotes in them contempt to God. He also tries to seduce the faithful if possible, & cautiously, making use of his slaves who under the shadow of some religion are branded to persuade the faithful of things which in appearance will seem simple. Once the Devil has won something from a man, this serves as a hook for him to gradually present himself & persuade a faithful man if no one prevents him from above. As for the principal means he uses to seduce men, the reader will see them in chapter 9 of our book entitled *De Spiritibus*.

The Devil creates such illusions in two principal ways. The first is by slipping to hide himself within the fantasy of men (if God by his special grace does not prevent him) in order to agitate the moods & disturb the senses by showing them strange things which are not real, as I have proved before, since in no way can he change the nature of things beyond the natural ability which the Creator has given them. On the other hand, some people will object that the same thing happens to these men but while they are asleep. The great fumes & vapors rising to the brain confuse the imaginative faculty & imprint diverse figures, which disappear after sleep & leave almost no trace in the memory. The imaginative faculty has been debilitated & something strange & frightful has imprinted itself on it in a way that people who had such visions remember them long afterwards if indeed such things happened.

Now, the variety of these visions are caused according to the diversity of the vapors, which are conditioned by the nature of the meat that is eaten, because if it is of difficult digestion, such as chestnuts, fish, pitch, celery, onions, leeks, cabbage, lentils, pork, beef, veal, goat meat, & other similar, which are those of which most Sorcerers feed, & with this the stomach is weakened as it usually happens with old women. Because of the natural heat, all meat is almost reduced to large & thick vapors which confuse the senses & hinder the intellectual faculty, that function which deals with the impressions, examines & distinguishes them to conclude which things are finally received by the imaginative in the common sense & return to the back part, where the Memorative faculty is located. The Memorative treasures the things learned from the Imaginative & concludes with the Cognitive or Raciocinium, with which they are faithfully stored. This is helped by the four states of mind, or complexions, & by the unreasonable fears or desires one person has for something. As for willingly, all that what we have heard & loved, or all what we greatly fear, or what we ardently desire during wakefulness, we see them while we sleep. Among the four complexions of men, melancholics are more likely to see strange things, both while sleeping & while they are awake, & the Devil takes benefits from this complexion & use it to frighten & make men fall into despair by reminding them of their sins as I shall prove for example in the book *De Veneficis*, at the chapter *Melancholics & Fools*.

This is what concerns natural causes, according to which we can see things that are not, & which, indeed, most of them have never existed, & that in some time afterwards we shall easily forget. Of these natural causes we have only spoken of melancholics & frantic people. Sometimes, however, the Devil intrudes into such moods or states of mind to try to seduce some & make others fall. Our objective is, therefore, to speak of Sorcerers & slaves of the Devil, whom the Devil persuades to such things by illusion, by disturbing their senses & altering their moods, or else by virtue of some ointment which he himself gives them to anoint their bodies. I will show later the proper & improper virtues of this ointment which is composed of material & natural things.

By means of natural matters & natural causes, nothing supernatural can be done, such as to say that by virtue of this ointment the soul is separated from the body without altering to its natural faculties, & returns then again to the body. To say that would be to disrupt the order of nature & confuse the natural with the divine, accusing God of blasphemy, or impotence, or, much worse, to be the author of evil as well as to allow the destruction of the order of Nature, which He himself has so closely established & preserved. But to His great honor & for the confusion of the wicked, we see how in the prayer of Joshua he simply stopped the Sun to destroy the enemies of his people, & in the death & passion of our Savior, he darkened & took away all the brightness of the Sun, as a sign of testimony to the divinity of our Savior, & of his wrath against the Jews who had crucified the King of glory, His beloved Son.

Judge then, dear reader, that it would be impiety to believe that God authorizes with his consent such an impious Serpent, jealous of his honor, & unwilling that His glory should be communicated to creatures like ourselves. As we may see in Herod, who, for having attributed to himself the glory, which is due to the one God, he was immediately devoured by lice in a just divine vengeance. What blasphemy, I would say, would it be to believe that God participated in the iniquities of the impious? He, who commands so strongly in the law, that such persons should be overthrown & put away from the face of the earth, for he not only abhors Sorcerers, Enchanters, Soothsayers, & Magicians, but also all those people who have recourse to them, & who believe in them.

Therefore, I believe it is quite clear that the Devil cannot separate the soul from the body & then return it to the body by any virtue, neither natural, nor even supernatural. Let us see now that such ointments, produced by his artifice, can be made naturally, since they are composed of basic things.

THE PLANTS INTO THE COMPOSITION OF THE OINTMENTS & THEIR GENERAL VIRTUES

.: CHAPTER TWO :.

Among all the plants which the Devil uses to disturb the senses of his slaves, the following appear to hold the first rank, of which all have the virtue to induce a profound sleep. The others have the property to confuse the senses by various figures & representations, both while being awake & during sleep. These are the Belladonna root, also called Morelle Furieuse (Furious Nightshade), bat & hoopoe blood, Aconite, Berula (Water Parsnip), the Sleeping Nightshade (la Morelle Endormante, Solanum nigrum), Umbellifers,

Soot, Cinquefoil, Acorum Vulgare, Parsley, the fronds of the White Poplar, Opium, Henbane, Hemlock & the Poppy species. Also, the Synochytides, which makes one see the shadow of Hell & the Evil Spirits, conversely to the Anachitides, which makes to appear images of Saints & the Holy Angels.

Of all these things the Devil is not satisfied, & as the enemy of the human race, in order to exercise his cruelty & tyranny, he persuades the Sorcerers to sacrifice small children for the purpose of extracting their grease, to make of it a broth to mix in the ointments. In reality, there is no truth found in consuming these infernal & diabolical compositions, merely they lead his slaves to the most enormous sin, & to the hatred of the human race, so that being immersed & overwhelmed in the abyss of their iniquity, they cannot hope for repentance, & perish with him.

So, then, of all the aforesaid things, with those oils or unguents, (not forgetting in this composition the particular invocation of the Demons, & the magical ceremonies instituted by them) all parts of the body were anointed until they turned red, so that the pores opened & thus the oil or ointment penetrated more strongly. These are the plants, besides several others, by which the understanding is so disturbed that the user will seem to be insane when speaking, while hearing or responding, or will fall into a deep sleep & remain insensitive for a few hours, or even a day. It must not be forgotten that in these things the Devil does not alter his personage. Now, it is not enough to simply describe things which have one or another virtue, if we do not demonstrate more particularly the triple usage of such ointments in order to better clarify this matter & avoid any doubt.

ON THE COMPOSITION &
USE OF THE FIRST OINTMENT
OF SORCERERS

.: CHAPTER THREE :.

WE HAVE SAID before that the Sorcerers who are distinguished or rather, those who belong to people of distinction & authority, do not dare to go to their Synagogues (Sabbaths) in body, for fear of being recognized by others, & being accused & defamed by a just punishment. In order to avoid this, the Devil, cautious & cunning, persuaded them saying that they would go there in spirit, on the condition that they anoint themselves with an ointment composed of his artifice, by virtue of which the soul would separate from the body for a few hours, & it would go to the place assigned by him. Their body would remain in their beds with their husbands, or other people, who were not aware of their absence. Let us examine the composition of such an ointment & see what it can do.

This one is composed of the grease of infants, the juice of the Water Parsnip, Aconite, Cinquefoil, Sleeping Nightshade, Black Mulberry & other similar herbs that have the somnolent virtue, & make them see strange things happening while sleeping. It is no wonder then, that after anointing with the ointment all parts of the body, & rubbing until they blush, it seems to them (to which they have their faith & intention) that they are borne in the air as the ointment penetrates & rises to the brain, & after he has entirely disturbed their senses & the ointment is fully ascended to the brain, the Devil fills it with diverse figures, so that they seem to see theaters, beautiful gardens, banquets, beautiful ornaments, vestments, Kings & Magistrates.

They also believe to hear music, to be at the dances, & to embrace the most beautiful young people that they desire. They also see the Devil, crows, prisons, deserts, storms, & they even see all the things that please them,

& they think that they enjoy or that they learn. These are the causes of these violent dreams, in which the sleepers are thought to be into diverse regions, & to have several affections according to the complexion of each of them & the intentions of the Devil, who achieves these things by the help of the ointment. To this, we may add that the effect of such violent & frequent impressions deprives the temperature of the brain so much, that even afterwards the spirit is altered by it, & day & night it does not think of anything other, & stays from the natural inclination in which it is accustomed to be. As a confirmation of this, we appeal to an example from Jean Baptiste Della Porta, a very learned man & a very subtle researcher of natural causes, added in his second book of *Natural Magic*.

"Unbridled greed," he said, "has so gained the understanding of men that even they abuse the things that nature has given them for their convenience. So much so that Witches compose ointments from many superstitious things, but whoever looks closely will see that the effects come from natural virtue." Having said this, he tells what he heard from them: "While I was endeavoring to discover these things more thoroughly (for I am still in doubt), I met a certain old woman of those who are known as Sorceresses & who suck the blood of little children in their cradles as it is said. This old woman, of her own free will, promised me that, shortly, she would give me an answer, ordering that everyone who came with me would leave, which they did. Shortly after, I saw through the slits in the door how she rubbed her entire body with an ointment. I watched as she fell to the ground by virtue of the ointment, & entered into a deep sleep, so finally the others arrived again, we opened the door & went inside. Then we started to shake her, but her sleep was so strong that she did not feel anything. Later, the strength of the ointment began to diminish & she woke up & told us several crazy things. She said that she had flown over the sea, & the mountains & she would say that she was telling us nothing false. We denied everything, but she would assure it even more. We would even show her the rub marks if she persisted."

It now remains to respond to an objection that we could make. It is known that we have observed several Sorcerers who were lying on the ground, or who were fast asleep on the ground by virtue of this ointment. If we look at them & watch them carefully, we see that, after a few hours, their spirit, as they said, returns in the form of an igneous fly, making a little noise as it enters, (because it enters through the mouth, which always remains half-open) & having entered, suddenly, the Sorcerer awakes. By this means several female suspects have already been discovered, & some have even been seen to be burned. To confirm the above, we maintain that, if we close the mouth so that there is no entrance, the spirit does not find the entrance, & after making some noises, it flutters around the head, turns around & no longer appears, so that the body dies & remains without movement.

Before answering this objection, we must know that since the Devil does nothing but stain the admirable works of our God through false miracles (by himself he does nothing real nor good, but only in appearance) in order to obscure & even annihilate, if possible, his glory. Also to do this, it is convenient for him (for fear that his blunders & deceptions will not appear) to keep men in ignorance, so that he may be glorified & admired by the ignorant. That is why we see some people in error to believe that souls can be separated from the body, & reintegrate it at the will of the Sorcerers. The Devil tries to confirm it with similar truths, but with demonstrations still very false, since the belief that the soul can be separated from the body & then re-enter after a few hours is false, as we have already proved. That this igneous fly that enters the Sorcerers is their soul is also false, because the soul is invisible. If it was corporeal, it would also necessarily be mortal, which is another falsehood, as I have shown extensively in our book *De Anima*. That the body of the witch awakens soon after the fly has entered concludes nothing, especially since it is not difficult for the Devil (as the virtue of the ointment is already beginning to diminish) to dissipate & expel the rest of the cerebral vapors, alter the moods, & stimulate the senses to perform their functions.

From all this, we conclude that it is the Devil, who under this form wants to deceive & bring the assistants in error, & by the same means authorizes the confession of his slaves. This form is very familiar to him, & even according to it he is called in the Holy Bible Beelzebub, or the Lord of the Flies, since we have never read that any good spirit has ever borrowed this form, nor from any other imperfect animal. As this objection is false, so is the proof.

We see how they naturally become drowsy from the narcotic vapors of this ointment. That is why the air that sometimes, without great attraction, maintains the vital spirits & lungs, is prevented by the closure of the ducts through which we sigh. & so, the body against the reversed nature, is easily deprived of the means by which it exercises its functions, & as every being disturbed by the great confusion which, in an instant, the vital spirits & narcotic vapors of these ointments have besieged the brain, it succumbs, & so the Sorcerer perishes, & the helpers end up being unthinkingly homicidal.

ON THE COMPOSITION &
USE OF THE SECOND OINTMENT
OF SORCERERS

.: CHAPTER FOUR :.

NOW, let us come to the second ointment, by which the Devil persuades the Witches, after being anointed, to stand upon a broom or a stick, to ride in the air & to go to their Synagogues with an incredible speed, passing up through the fireplace. What Cardan & Giambattista della Porta dealt with lightly, other men denied, together with some scholars, stating that this was not an illusion caused by the virtues of the ointments, which I dare to deny & prove the opposite. I firstly deny that this is caused without the virtue of the ointment, but the Devil wants the witches to use it in order to disturb their senses, to be at his service & become so stupefied that they would do what otherwise, being in their right mind, they would not dare to undertake or even think about. Not that they are evil per se, but the memory of those things when they come back to them make them most of the time so confused that they dare not look at good people in the eyes. So, they walk with their heads down, especially because they are ashamed & cannot sustain the constant gaze of good people without lowering their gaze, & that is why they are flatulent, bigoted, lonely, superstitious, ugly, stinking & dirty.

Now, before moving forward, it should be noted that no simple narcotics are used in the composition of this ointment but only those which have the virtue to disturb the senses by alienating them, as for example, wine taken excessively, Belladonna, cat brains & other things that I keep silent about in order to not give the wicked an opportunity to do evil with this information. This transport is not done merely by the illusions of profound sleep, as we have observed in the discourse of the virtues of the first ointment through natural causes, but also, really, not by the virtues of the ointment, but by the help of the Devil who carries them away in a pleasant daydream, just as he carries the Magicians through the air.

For it is to be noted that the Devil can do this since God has already reproved such persons, so that, being slaves of the Devil, he can carry them through the air with astonishing speed. I cannot believe, therefore, that anyone is so lacking in sense as to deny that a body cannot be lifted up from the earth to be carried through the air. Because, although the Devil has fallen from the Grace of God by his pride, yet he can do much considering the nobility, excellence, & power of the nature which he has received. It is not that this power extends over the good, but on the contrary & with respect to others, is limited & restrained, in an extraordinary way. As when God wanted to test the patience of Job, he gave Satan free rein to afflict him with the loss of his property & his children as long as he did not harm his life. Therefore, it is not of this power that we speak, but of the one which the Devil absolutely has over the wicked while they are in a state of damnation, & before they have repented & converted to the Lord, after what it then ceases.

Returning to the transportation of Sorcerers, we will add that it is a mockery of the Evangelical History to question whether the Devil transports the sorcerers from one place to another, since we read in the Gospel that Satan transported our Lord Jesus Christ to the pinnacle of the Temple, & over the top of the mountain. In the same way as the Angel carried the prophet Habakkuk to Babylon. & as Elijah & Enoch were taken to heaven in their body & soul, & with an infinity of other such examples. Among the most outstanding one is that of Apollonius of Tiara who, as we can read from Philostratus, a Greek author, was transported in only a few hours, from Ethiopia, near the source of the Nile, to Rome. In the same way, he was also transported from Rome to Corinth & finally once again from Smyrna to Ephesus.

We also read that, in 1271, Jean Teuthonich, priest of Albartard, one of the most famous sorcerers of his time, sang three Masses at midnight. One was in Albartard, the second in Mainz & the third in Cologne. Plutarch also mentions a similar transport made from Greece to Croton, near Naples. What is also said of Pythagoras is that he was transported from Thussia to Metapontum, & in the last days of Faustus, he was transported with some others from Basel in Switzerland, to Rome. Similarly, there was another transport of a Magician from Burgundy to Bordeaux. Here we could add a great number of such & similar transports made in our time, both in Savoy, Switzerland, Germany, France, Spain & Italy, but the topic is clear enough by itself.

I do not think that anyone doubts this anymore, since all the ancient Theologians corroborate it when they say that the Devils, with the forces of their nature & with the permission of God, can make things have a local motion, with a proper knowledge of active & passive things. But always remembering that, in no way, they can change the nature of things against the natural ability that the Creator has given them. As a proof & confirmation of the transport of the Sorcerers in body & soul, I will add, before closing this chapter, the story of a transport made in our time, which seemed to me among a million worthy to be brought to light so that the curious may learn to restrain themselves within the limits of reason & not to inquire with too much curiosity about illicit things that can only bring & cause misfortune, being forbidden by God & by His Word, which is the only one that must be followed.

In the month of August of the year 1603, while residing at Anaut, a famous city about four hours from Frankfurt, ulcers appeared on my feet with a large edematous tumor which increased every hour. I was obliged to call in a certain young man from Frankfurt, a jovial surgeon as humorous as possible, but who had been very curious. From his own mouth he told me a curious story, which goes as follows:

Having heard so often about the Sorcerers going by night through the air to their Synagogues, where they danced, jumped, feasted, shouted & accounted for the evil they committed at the instigation of their master, this surgeon had a great desire to find a way to go there to find out the truth of these things. He decided to talk to his aunt in Frankfurt, who was suspected to be a Witch, & urged her to confess the truth to him, which she flatly refused & even threatened him. But he, out of the extreme desire he had to satisfy his damned curiosity, did not allow the threats to disturb him & begged her to confess the truth with protests & oaths not to unmask her. She, at last, pressed & constrained by his prayers & unwanted requests, confessed that she was a Witch. The young man, not yet content, asked her when would she go to the

Synagogue, to which with some difficulty she replied that it would be next Thursday. Having understood this, her nephew did not desist until he had obtained something from her; either that she would allow him to go together, or that he would be at her house on the night of her departure. In the end, he was refused to go along with her, but was granted to be at her departure.

Thursday night arrived, at about eleven o'clock she left her nephew & went into another room with light, where she undressed & took an ointment which she had hidden, with which (after having rubbed her whole body well) she anointed herself. She then put a broom between her legs, & having done this, disappeared being carried in the air four leagues away from Frankfort towards the Rhine.

This young man having secretly spied on her & watched everything she did by looking through a hole in the door, suddenly entered the room after she had disappeared & he did the same as she did. The Devil, in the form of a whirlwind also took him by the chimney & carried him to the same place where his aunt was, who upon recognizing him was very much astonished, & approached him to learn how he had come there, to which he answered her frankly. She told him not to be in any way afraid of the man who stood in their midst dressed in black, and, for greater safety, told him to remain silent, & greased the tip of his broom with an ointment that the Devil had given her. Now, as they dance in a circle, this poor man was astonished & the Devil looked at him with such apprehension that the hairs on his head stood on end, but he was forced to keep a nice face, for fear of becoming a prey. The assembly ended two hours after midnight & the Devil led them all, as before, to the Rhine.

The Devil took the form of a calf & carried them all away one after the other. This time the aunt approached her nephew, still a young apprentice of demonology, & ordered him not to be afraid, but to boldly ride on this calf without saying a word. The aunt passed by, & with only the nephew being left to mount, the calf approached him & got mounted by him on the bank of the Rhine, & in order to mock him & punish him by a just permission of God for his detestable curiosity, he threw the nice horseman into the middle of the Rhine, & screamed in irritation: "What a nice jump from a calf". The surgeon was very surprised and, after having swallowed a lot of water, tried to save himself by swimming. But he had a hard time, for the Rhine with its speed carried him a league away near a mill, where he was seen that day by the miller, who with a small skiff tried to save him & pull him out of the water, since he was more dead than alive. Once this was done, the miller & his servants hung him by his feet to make him release the water he had swallowed in excess. At last, coming to his senses little by little, having recovered his speech & regained his strength, he told the whole story & promised with oaths to put an end to all his curiosities by asking God's forgiveness for the past, with promises that he would live more prodigiously in the future. Once in Frankfurt, he denounced his aunt, but she was not burned, as the authorities now believed it to be fables & reveries. He added that, moreover, a good part of the wealthier people would have an interest in this whole subject, of whom suspicion is cast upon them & were singled out.

This is the story that this surgeon told me & confirmed with oaths in the presence of people of honor, in which we can highlight four notable things: confirming his damned curiosity, the wiles of the Devil, the punishment of the curious, & the mercy of God which he showed by miraculously saving & freeing this man, both from the clutches of the Devil & from the deep waters, into which he had been thrown to lose & drown him. God had mercy on him at the moment of his death, not wanting to destroy this young man. Therefore, we must learn that it is He alone who can save soul & body, for He is the author of life, & that the Devil only has power over the bodies of the ungodly who are in a state of perdition.

The Devil can play with them, ruin them, tyrannize them for a limited time, for he has no power over their lives, because God shows mercy to whom he pleases, even at the moment of death. Thus, He brings from death to life those whom, by a particular & special grace, He wants to save, not wanting the death of the sinner, but rather wanting him to repent & to be converted to Him. The Devil is only the executor of high Justice to punish in this world, whether in body or in goods, those who have sinned against the living God, who never allows such enormous wickedness to go unpunished, & although He sometimes seems to dilute the punishment, we already know that, either in this world or in the next, we shall not escape His just punishment. So let the curious learn to put an end to their infamous curiosity, & to be soberly wise, lest something similar to what happened to the surgeon should befall them, or even worse, if God did not have mercy on them.

Nam facilis descensus Averni, Sed revocare gradum, superasq; evadere ad auras, Hoc opus, hic labor est.

Easy is the descent to Avernus, for the door to the underworld lies open both day & night. But to retrace your steps & return to the breezes above... that is the task, that is the toil.

For it is not in the power of man, after he has fallen into the clutches of the Devil, to come out of it by himself if God, by a special grace, does not extend his hand to withdraw him, since repentance is a special gift of God. But who can promise that God will give them repentance after they have turned their backs on him & despised his word? Who has mercy on God? Let us therefore adhere to Him alone & to His Word, because without it there is only death & condemnation.

ON THE COMPOSITION & USE OF THE THIRD OINTMENT OF SORCERERS

.: CHAPTER FIVE :.

We have already discovered at considerable length the appropriate & inadequate virtues of the first & second ointments which the Sorcerers used in order to go, either in body or in spirit, to their nocturnal assemblies. Finally, it remains to speak of the third ointment that the Devil gives to the Sorcerers, persuading them that after they have been anointed, they would be transformed into beasts, & thus they will be able to conquer the fields.

As for the reality of the Sorcerers & their sacrileges on the glory of God, I have amply demonstrated that it can only be achieved through diabolical illusions. But now let us see if is possible that, naturally, by means of some ointments or potions, the understanding of a man can be so perverted that he believes himself to be truly transformed into a beast.

As for ointments, they may be composed of certain parts taken from a toad, a serpent, a hedgehog, a wolf, a fox, human blood, etc. All this was mixed with plants, roots & other similar things, which have the virtue of disturbing the imagination. For, as I have said, the Devil always makes use of Sorcerers through ingested substances taken internally, or else applied externally. Having the spirit & the senses disturbed by the figures of such animals, they think they take the form of some of them. As the Devil has persuaded them, the Evil Spirit enter into them in order to perfect his willpower & he lead them into error by counterfeiting the illusory forms of the beasts, which they borrow. For instance, if they are in the shape of a wolf, they run through the woods, they rush upon other animals, more often, upon unarmed men & infants that they rip & devour, as I shall show an instance of the abduction of a child which took place in the year 1604 in a village called Cressi, distant about a league from the city of Lausanne.

The story goes as follows:

A villager threshing corn in his barn was bothered by his little boy who asked for a drink, to which the father paid no attention because of his dedication to his work. The little boy started to press harder for a drink with tears & screams. The father became irritated & threatened the child who did not stop but, on the contrary, increased his tears & crying. In the end, the father overcome with anger said to him in these own words, "May the Devil drink you". This pronouncement came a few days before the action took place on Friday, one day after the Synagogue was held according to their custom. The Devil, by a just punishment & permission from God (who, as I said before, never leaves such great sins unpunished) gathered five Witches, to whom he communicated his wish by such ointments & who in the form of wolves abducted the child in broad daylight. Then, they took the little boy to the place where their accomplices were waiting for them, & where they took back the form of women, & the Devil, in the presence of them all, sucked all the blood of this child through the great toe of his foot. He, then, cut the body into pieces to boil it in a cauldron, of which they ate one part, & with the other one they composed their own ointment along with other things. Later, the five Witches confessed, being arrested by justice & taken to Lausanne, where I saw them being burned & judged.

The second story is that of a peasant from a village near Lucens in Switzerland, who found himself in the middle of the forest where a hungry wolf began to run to devour him. Seeing this, the peasant got defensive & managed to cut off one of its forelegs, which made blood spill & the wolf soon transform into a woman who, instead of an animal leg, had now a cut off arm. The peasant came back to his village & accused the woman, & she was soon arrested & burned. In connection with this story, it will not be considered bad if we publish a maxim which is held among the Vaudois & which is confirmed by the confession of an infinite number of Witches. It is to be known that, as soon as Witches transform into beasts, when they are wounded, as soon as the shedding of blood follows the wound, their illusory form disappears, & they are recognized for what they are, that is, women or men. In addition to this, there are two other maxims known about these people transformed into animals:

The first one is, that all the Witches transformed into beasts by diabolical illusions have no tails. The second is that the Devil can never take the form of anything that resembles a man, & that all the infamous Witches & Magicians agree, for they confess that even if the Devil would take the form of a man, they could recognize him by his feet, which cannot change to any other form than that of beasts, such as goats, oxen, & other animals. They also recognize him by his nails, which are long & hooked. & also, according to their statements & strictly speaking, the Devil has no body, especially because he is all Spirit.

As to the reality of this metamorphosis of men into beasts, I have sufficiently proven above that it could not really be done by any natural way, not even by the Devil, even if he would employ all his strength in it. Because, this power only belongs to the one God, Creator & Preserver of all that is & moves.

Some still not satisfied with the reasons & arguments alleged above, will justify themselves by saying that this metamorphosis cannot be fantastic or made merely by illusion, but that there is reality, since it does not happen only to the Witches who have anointed themselves with ointments or taken some potion with which they seem to transform themselves into beasts, but also to those who look at them whose senses are deranged, since they have taken neither ointment nor potion.

This objection would not deserve a particular response, since it is comprised in what I have already answered, in addition to the fact that no one ignores that the Devil cannot dazzle the eyes of men, & make things appear which are not real, as Charmers usually do. Normally they use natural substances, such as eye drops, ointments, potions, & perfumes, made & composed of certain special ingredients, as we shall demonstrate at the end of this chapter.

But before going further, to satisfy the doubters, it is necessary to answer this objection, & to distinguish the illusion of the spectators from that of the Witches metamorphosed in their imaginations. For the illusion of those who observe such monsters is only external, & is caused by a single sense, through the eyes, that see a phantom in the form of a beast, & they believe that it is a real beast. & the eyes, such deceived, represent it as such for the common sense, & from the common sense it passes to the cognitive sense, & finally the cognitive sense returns it to the memory.

But the illusion & impression of the Witches themselves is much greater, especially since all their senses, both internal & external, are deceived by another means which does not deceive the eyes of the beholders. Because, in the first place, their inner senses are disturbed by violent impressions of a vain figure, & they are even driven from such a fury, by ointments or potions, which naturally excite them so that they believe themselves to be veritable beasts. Thus, they lay down on the ground in the manner of beasts, & use their hands as forefeet. Finally, being thus disposed, the Devil surrounds them in a thick air, which outwardly represents to all spectators the figure of a wolf and, thus, carries the Witches under this form over hills & valleys, because men can only see the Devil in some bodily or phantom form.

So, in the story of Saint Clement, we read that Simeon the Magician made sure that all the friends of Faustino did not know him, then he told Nero the Emperor to cut off his head, assuring him that he would be resurrected on the third day, & so Nero did. Three days later he came back to life, & Nero, surprised, made a statue to the magician in Rome with such an inscription: *Simoni Deo Santo Mago* (to Simon the Holy Magician) & after that Nero devoted himself entirely to witchcraft. Simon the Magician had so fascinated the eyes of Nero & the entire assembly that they carried out the sacrifice of a sheep in honor to Simon.

Apuleius recites something similar about three men he thought he had killed, who were transformed into rams by the Witch Pamphila. I have seen the same thing so many times with Charmers, who practiced with bloodshed (as the spectators seemed to see) of little children, whom after taking the head, which seemed to be separated from the body, arranged it joint against joint & nerve against nerve. After having performed some ceremonies, & having done so, the child would suddenly stand up strong & in good shape.

Also, a good man, called de la Pierre, from the city of Grand-Son, in Switzerland, sold at the market of Hyuerdon straw corks & pigs to the Burgundians. When the pigs were sold, the man who sold them forbade the Burgundians to take them down a stream between Hyuerdon & Grand-Son. But in spite of the prohibition, the Burgundians led them along the stream & when they entered in it, the pigs disappeared & they saw only straw plugs that the current was carrying away. Seeing this, with much astonishment, they returned to Hyuerdon, to the lodging where Monsieur de la Pierre was staying who, in the meantime, had lain down on a bed where he seemed to be sleeping soundly.

The Burgundians arrived, & the servant-maid went up to the room to wake him up, but having failed to wake him up with her words, she was forced to pull one of his legs with great force, so much that she took it with her being, according to her, separated from his body. Very distressed, she thought she had killed him, so, to be sure, she wanted to look at his face, which was turned on the other side. She decided to turn his head to see his face, & suddenly, she was left with his head in her hands, totally separated from his body, or so it seemed to her. She cried & screamed thinking that she had completely killed him, so she went downstairs & told her owner. But the owner of the house, seeing her crying like that when she went out, wanted to know the cause of it, to which she answered with great difficulty, so the owner decided to go upstairs to the room to find out the truth of what was happening. Being upstairs, she found Pierre awake wandering about the room, so that the tears were changed to laughter, & he returned the money to the Burgundians.

The same thing happened at the wedding feast of a certain gentleman, where there were several ladies & maidens dancing alone in a separate room, beating a small drum which was kept for this purpose. At the first sound, the ladies believed it to be the sound of a stream which they saw at that moment instantly emerge from the wall, which as it seemed to them, became larger & louder as the drum was beaten harder. The ladies who seemed as if enchanted & bewitched, gradually lifted up their dresses for fear of getting them wet, finally the stream grew larger & larger, until they were forced to lift their dresses & shirts up to their navels, which pleased the man & the spectators who were with him. In the end, he had the water reduced little by little until it disappeared completely. Because if he had continued increasing it, the ladies would have been terrified, & perhaps fainted for fear of drowning.

There was another good man who was only engaged in passing the time pleasantly. Once, going to see his servants in the height of the day, he gave them the alarm to flee, rebuking them very bitterly for their negligence, as they clearly saw the enemy at their heels. The servants, very much astonished, looked behind them & saw a very numerous army, (it seemed to them in appearance to see soldiers & pikemen) so, in great fear, they all rose to their feet & departed without stopping until they reached the city, where everyone were basically making fun of them.

Thus was a Monk also deceived (as Saint Jerome tells us in *La Vie des Pères* in chapter 28) when he saw the Devil in the form of a beautiful woman who often tempted him to the venereal act, to which the poor Monk wanted to comply. Instead of that, he was transformed into something similar to a horse or a mule that had no understanding. While he tried to kiss her to take carnal pleasure with her, this phantom, which was nothing but a shadow that slipped from his arms with a horrible bellow, left the poor wretch with great mockery.

In this way Luciano was transformed into a donkey & became a man again after having eaten the roses that a servant had shown him. Thus, Apuleius was also transformed into a donkey & the Arcades into wolves. Those who, as Saint Augustine tells us, had eaten the poisoned swarm by the cattle guardians experienced in this art were transformed into horses & donkeys, carrying the burdens that horses are accustomed to carry, & immediately afterwards they returned to their human nature.

This was done by the Devil to make use of his lie & deception. Because, as Saint Augustine very wisely said in the *City of God*, "neither the spirit of man, nor his body, can be truly (as I also showed above) transformed by art, nor by the power of the Devil into limbs nor into lineages of beasts, since demons cannot create nature. The only thing they can do is to make a thing appear as what it is not." Let us now leave the wiles & impostures of the Devil, & try to show that, naturally, & without any artifice of the Demons, we can see or make things appear to be, as they are not. Let us begin first with Lycanthropy.

ON NATURAL LYCANTHROPY

.: CHAPTER SIX :.

NATURAL LYCANTHROPY is a disease that some people call *Melancholy*, or *Lupine Madness* & others call it *Lycaonia*, or *Cynanthropy*, because those who have this disease think they are transformed into wolves, or dogs. This happens to them through the fumes of melancholy, or black rage, that rises to the brain & disturbs all the senses & mainly the imaginative, which is disturbed. For that reason, they believe they hear & see outside, what is actually inside & consists of the smoke & vapors of the brain, so that the errors caused by the disease of the imaginative, depraved by such smokes & vapors, are translated & sent outside. It is for that reason that werewolves leave their home mainly at night, & follow wolves, like the *sinanthropus* follow the dogs. They are pale & have sunken & tormented eyes. They see in a blurred manner, as if they were surrounded by darkness. Their tongues are very dry & they are thirsty & they do not even have saliva in their mouth. They also have very badly scratched leg bones, because they often bump/collide with others, & dogs bite them, so it is very difficult to cure them. The cure for such a disease is almost similar in everything to that of the maniacs or melancholics, that is already explained in the book entitled, *de Veneficis*. Thus, Lycaon, King of Arcadia (from whose name also comes the word Lycaonia) because of his wickedness, was transformed into a wolf by Jupiter, as Ovid wrote in the first book of his *Metamorphoses* in which he said:

Terror struck he took to flight, & on the silent plains is howling in his vain attempts to speak.

I can affirm this because the Devil cannot make such things appear for so many days in a row, neither can potions, collyriums or ointments which last only a few days. When the force of these means is dissolved, either the man returns to his natural state & survives by nature, or else the man dies defeated by the violence of such compositions. This may occur because all that is violent cannot subsist/persist for long in the same degree.

Avicenna, a very famous doctor among the Arabs, also noted that in these states tormented by this anger they are believed to be lions, devils, or birds, as we have alleged several examples in the chapter on Mania, or melancholy fury, in the book de Veneficis. Now let us see whether by means of potions, collyriums, & unctions we can make such or similar things appear.

ON NATURAL THINGS
HAVING CERTAIN IMAGINARY
VIRTUES NOT PRESENT IN EFFECT
BUT ONLY IN APPEARANCE

.: CHAPTER SEVEN :.

Just as the senses of the Lycanthropes or Cynanthropes aforesaid are naturally deceived & confused by the virtue of the inner vapours & fumes exhaled by their fury in their brain, in the same way they can also be deceived by potions & powders that they take internally, or by eye drops, anointing, & perfumes taken externally, composed of herbs, fruits seeds, roots, juices, woods & some parts of certain animals, which have the virtue of disturbing & deceiving the senses, & make appear to them vain figures of things that are not really present.

With similar ingredients, the Turks composed a certain powder they called *Heiranluc* (that I will not speak of for the present) which, taken by the weight of a drachm or about, caused them to loose speech, & then immediately made them laugh & being joyous. The persons believed they were experiencing beautiful & pleasant things, & for that reason would make any gestures with their body [assisted with a great laughter], & then, coming back to their senses, would relate that they had been to various places, & that they had seen great & wonderful things.

We also attribute the same virtues or similar ones to *Geotephillide* (possibly Centipede), when it is taken with wine & myrrh. The *Stramonium* & the *Solanum* do the same, & so does the species called by the Italians *Belladonna*, & several others whose use & composition I will not speak of, because I do not want to give opportunity to the wicked to do evil things by their depraved actions. Baptiste Porta the Neapolitan tells us in the eighth book of his *Natural Magic* that some of his friends were capable of alienating the sensual perceptions of a man with a certain potion in order to persuade him to metamorphose into a bird or another animal. This was in accordance with the variable composition of such potions. They once made one by virtue of which the person who had taken was convinced that he was transformed into a fish so, while on the ground, he stretched his arms & moved his legs as if he was about to swim. Sometimes he also quivered, trembling, & it seemed to him as if he was submerged. They also made another potion which alienated the person from his senses so much that he was completely persuaded that he was transformed into a goose, pecking at the grass with its mouth, & hitting the ground with its teeth, in the manner of a goose. He also sang & sprang about in his movements.

Touching on the subject of mesmerism, Jules Scalinger & Mathiole tell a remarkable story of some conjurers. They say that they mixed the powder of a certain root, which was spicy to the palate, in wine. Once it is done, they order a person to dip his finger in this wine & suck it in order to tell how it tastes like. As soon as he dipped it & put it in his mouth, he is forced to squeeze & bite it with loud cries. On the other hand, the Bateleur, pretending to console him, rubs his wrist & temples of the man with a certain ointment, then takes a silver coin, intentionally let it fall & ask his victim to pick it up. Having lowered himself down, the man cannot rise again, & by virtue of the ointment becomes insensate, he falls flat on the ground, & in the same way as someone who believes to have taken the form of a fish, he swims, & cries that the waters are carrying him away. The Bateleur stands him up, to which he begins to look askance at him & reproaches him for these outrages. He then appears to run at the conjurers & chase them, which continues until the effect of the ointment wears off. Once this is done, he comes to his senses, & suddenly, like one who has escaped from drowning, he wrings his hair, his beard & his clothes, dries his arms & flees.

Now, I assure you that we can do certain things which I have described above (regarding the composition of the Sorcerers ointments). Like special potions by virtue of which one will appear to be transformed into the animal whose arteries, heart & brain will have been mixed in the said potion. In case we cannot dispose of these parts of the animal we wish to make appear, we can simply feed the person to whom we wish to give such a potion with the flesh of the animal to which we wish him to be transformed by means of imagination, & after a few hours of giving him the potion we shall see the effect. Thus, if he has eaten ox meat, he will see only oxen & will believe that he has become one, so that he will want to fight with his horns as oxen normally do. Thus, Pliny writes that the brain of a Bear, being consumed by a human agitates the imagination & one becomes ferocious, while one is transformed into a bear, & this without feeling any harm afterwards. This is something that claim to have experienced a Spanish gentleman, who after tasting this delicacy had such a disturbed fantasy that, he was thinking himself to be a bear & lost himself in the woods believing himself to be such an animal.

On this subject, a certain scholar writes in some of his books that it is possible to perform certain anointings which force sleepers to speak, walk & do things which they cannot do & which they would not even dare to undertake when they are awake. As proof of this, he says that he knows how to make eye drops with the skin of a man, the eyes of a black cat & some other things he does not name, that will make the shadows of the Demons appear in the air. The same author, speaking of perfumes, says that if one perfumes himself with Linseed, & Psyllium with Violet & Parsley roots, he will see things from the future, in the same way as if we make a perfume with Bruyere (Heather), the juice of Hemlock, Henbane, & Black Poppy seeds with some other things that will cause to see very strange figures. To drive away Evil Spirits & phantoms, make a perfume of calamon, peony, mint & Palma Christi. He also teaches that in order to attract serpents, one will burn the windpipe of a stag, & to expel them, burn a horn of the same animal. The serpents can appear due to the perfume of the bones of the extremity of the throat of the deer, & in this way, we can hunt them if we burn the horn of the deer itself. In the same way, the horse hoof of a horse or a mule burned in a house drives away mice, & that of the left paw scares away flies. He also says that, if a perfume is created with gall of fish, thyme, roses & aloe wood, & that when it is finished you add water or blood, the house will seem to be full of water or blood, & on the contrary, if plowed earth is poured on it, it will seem that the whole earth begins to tremble.

This is what I wanted to write to show how great the forces of nature are, & how vain, even detestable, is the presumption of these stupid writers. These, who, for not being able to hear & understand the great secrets of the virtues of Nature which God has given to the creatures that are under the concavity of the heavens, let themselves go by their brutal ignorance when they see something happen in an extraordinary manner. They relate these causes to demons, not without great impiety, because in doing so they seem to want to establish a second Deity. Therefore, it is not surprising that those ignorant of the causes of things believe in such absurdities, into which they would not have fallen if they had not put science & doctrine into vain palaver. Because true science is based on the knowledge of the causes that depend on a single causative cause, which is God, who in creation assigned to each creature, according to species & dignity, a particular power which they cannot exceed.

According to these properties & virtues given to each species, Adam imposed their names on them to distinguish them from one another. Moreover, we must believe that since God is the author of all things, he is also the sole preserver & protector, having reserved to him this prerogative of creating, giving life, & transforming forms into others. In short, He can do what he wills with his creatures, because it is He alone who made them & molded them so that he could either change or destroy them. With these foundations presented as impregnable, it will be easy to reverse the arguments of these turbulent people. But returning to our subject, when they hear through the confessions of Sorcerers that the they turn into wolves or other animals, they not only believe it, but maintain that it is done by the Devil with the permission of God. Now, before hastening their judgment, it would be necessary first to note whether it can be done in this way or in an illusory manner.

According to the veracity of our foundations & arguments mentioned above, it cannot be done by any natural cause or power of the Devil, that a body is truly transformed into another species. From this we conclude, then, that it is done illusorily. That if, considering that God has never permitted miracles, it would be necessary now to believe indifferently that He does & permits them, there would be no firm & stable faith, & all things would have to be put in doubt, even the articles of faith, which are the foundation of what we hope for, & the certification of the things which we do not see, as St. Paul says in Hebrieux in chapter 10.

Moreover, if I wanted to grant that all things are or happen on the premise that God can do anything, I should have to believe in some surprising cases. Even if from such an argument, (what God did, or can do, is therefore, what God does) there were sufficient cause & reason for what God to do them, all Philosophy & disputes of divine things would perish in to the extent that God can make new things & destroy old & ancient ones. What if we had to believe all things, as the Poet Linus wants, because all things are possible to God? Certainly, all science, both divine & human would perish, & all means of discerning the false from the true would be excluded from us. Especially as we would be compelled to believe stranger & greater things than we could understand, & most of the time lies would be taken for truth. Because the omnipotent power of God would force us to do so, despite the fact that our senses & our reason refuses it. You just have to look at the Holy Bible.

That is why today we see people of great wisdom & reputation do not estimate miraculous & supernatural works. Putting them in perspective with the knowledge in the natural sciences, they find a rightful reason to not attribute diseases to demons, knowing their cause is purely natural. For the rest, I do not want to deny that God through the faith of his servants performed many miracles, & that He did not allow Evil Spirits & Magicians to do so, for having done many admirable & wonderful is to his honor, for the salvation of the good & the blindness of the castaways, & not the other way around.

That if Evil Magicians, or miserable Sorcerers confess & claim to have done dreadful things, we should not believe them because they have not really done all that they think & believe. All this is confirmed in the canon *Episcopi eorumque ministri*, where it says in substance:

"When Satan takes possession of the head of a woman, & subjugates her to himself through infidelity, becoming suddenly in the likeness of several persons, & lulling her spirit, he holds it captive, showing her monstrous things, as well as sad things, then beating people, he drags her confused from here to there. & whatever the spirit endures & suffers, the unbeliever thinks that it does not happen to the spirit, but to the body."

If we come to deny the above things saying that according to them we ought not to believe in any miracle, we respond that the consequence is not good & valid, considering that there is no miracle without cause & reason, & that there is nothing better than the faith in our Lord Jesus Christ, by whom they are really done. The Church does not need miracles, because the Christian faith is sufficiently approved & confirmed, both by miracles & martyrdoms, by great & very wise figures who have undoubtedly consented to it after countless trials & questions.

So there are no more miracles, & if there are, they are done immediately by God or through his Saints, Angels & Servants, all for his honor & glory, to be admired & feared, even more so when we are too cowardly & reluctant to do our duty. From which we conclude that it is heresy, even blasphemy, to say that God gives such extraordinary power to the Devil, or that through Him he exhibits these miracles, which are but to confirm evil-doers in the servitude of the devil, & to authorize his abominable & execrable assemblies convened in contempt of God & His word, & for the destruction of the human race. Would this not make God the author of iniquity & the destroyer of his own glory? God, who is the author of Justice & all good, & who has in store vengeance & glory over all things. Therefore, God is not a participant in the iniquities of the ungodly, as those who maintain such metamorphoses & ecstasies as real would like to infer.

REFUTATION
of the opinions & arguments of Jean Bodin in the Sixth Chapter of his Demonomania maintaining the reality of the Lycanthropy of Sorcerers

.: CHAPTER EIGHT :.

It is not enough to have previously demonstrated above that the transformation of men into beasts & the transport of the soul outside the body of witches are only fables & pure illusions of the Devil, if we do not also refute the main arguments, on which those who maintain that such things were real, among whom Bodin occupies the first place. That is why we will now refute his opinions & arguments that he alleges, protesting without being driven to do so by ambition, nor by any hatred. But only to maintain the honor of God against which he seems to have wished to arm himself to give the belief such detestable &

ridiculous things to those who might have been seduced by his arguments, whose falsehood I will show by turning them against him.

He & his followers, being poorly instructed both in the Christian faith & in natural philosophy, cannot admit that this is in an illusory form. Being too credulous, they assure that such a transformation is really wrought by the Devil, urging it again because of the Devil's impotence, he has recourse to the permission of God, by which they discover more & more their ignorance. Now the Devil has never had the power to do such things, neither before his fall nor afterwards, therefore, it follows that this permission is null & void. Putting the case that God permitted it, or does not prevent it (if it is necessary to speak like that) he could not execute it because he does not have the power to do it, & he cannot go beyond the power that he received at the beginning, he cannot even do what he, according to the nature of his essence, could.

Because the Devil lost his free will & is restricted, so that he can do nothing by himself if God does not permit him to do so. But according to this permission, the Devil could not do any of the above things, so this conclusion is false & inept. What is more ridiculous than constructing an argument about someone's inability to do something, & then later attributing power to them to do the same thing previously stated? Is it not that deceiving yourself, & making sure that cold is heat & that heat is cold? Here, then, they will have to confess having sinned through ignorance or malice, or else, to crown their blasphemy by saying that God gives such extraordinary power to the Devil.

In all this we will note three absurdities, damnable heresies, which are the following: The first is to accuse God of favoring the Devil more than the Angels & any other creature, because we do not read in the Holy Bible that God has ever given this or that power to any creature. The second is to tacitly accuse God of being the destroyer of his own glory, of which the Devil himself so expressly said to be jealous, & that he does not want to communicate it to creatures. The third is to accuse God of authorizing sin by confirming it with miracles that completely surpass the nature of the good & evil spirits that he always teaches us to abhor.

From all this, we conclude that it is blasphemy to assert that God allows or gives such power to the Devil, enemy of his word & of the human race as Bodin maintains in the second book of his Demonomania in chapter 6. Here, he cites as irrelevant evidence the passage from Job, who says that there is no power so great on earth that can resist the Devil. The reason for this is very obvious, especially since he received a spiritual essence that is above the elemental, but this does not mean that God gave him the power to change bodies. Seeing that Job speaks only of the power he received in his creation, that is still limited by the will of God, because of the elect, who can resist to it by the word of God.

Therefore, this passage extracted from Job concludes nothing, nor do the others that he quotes & falsely corrupts, which, in order that the truth may be more evident, I will refute one after another beginning with that of Nebuchadnezzar, which Bodin asserts to have been really metamorphosed into an ox, which (even if that would be so) cannot conclude anything. This is because, if the transformations were true, it would have been done by God as the demonstrable voice from heaven & not by Satan, of whom no mention is made. It should be added that

Daniel does not say that he was really transformed into an ox, but only speaks of a comparison, saying that he ate grass like oxen, & adds that the hair of the body was so long that it seemed to him like the hair of eagles & his nails like those of birds.

Therefore, we see that he was not really an ox, but that he resembled an ox because he was eating grass & living in the forest with animals. & that he also resembled with his great hair to an eagle & that his nails sembled those of the birds, it does not mean that he was an eagle or a bird. Even less that he was really an ox, although he thought he was, since he had the heart & sense of an ox. Only God could really turn him into an ox or a stone, or even reduce him to anything since the Creator can do what He wills with His creatures. Even when God wants to punish & overthown men, He usually does so by disease, famines & war, as we see in the Psalms of David, to whom God gave the choice between these three plagues. Because through them he brought down the pride & ambition of the great, as we see in Herod, who, for not having given glory to God, were wounded with a particular disease, Saul by war, Israel by famine, & Egypt by water.

So, it is credible that Nebuchadnezzar, for having attributed to himself the glory due to the one God, was struck by divine vengeance with this kind of melancholy or bovine madness. Because of this, in an instant his senses became so disturbed that he believed himself to be an ox & became quadrupedal, deprived of the functions of the intellectual soul. Therefore, people seeing a so sudden a change & after having heard from Heaven that he was to be expelled from the company of men, we are not surprised that he was expelled, for such was the divine decree.

What Daniel also seems to explain when he said that seven years had passed, he lifted up his eyes to heaven & his understanding was restored to him afterwards, we clearly see that he was not actually an ox, but a man. However, he was deprived of the functions of reason for a time which, having expired, made the disease also cease, so that, beginning to be known as a man again, he found himself with the voice of the Lord. His bovine life, which, compared with his greatness & first magnificence, was nothing but abjection & brutality, recognized that a change so sudden & so great could not have been made but by a supreme God, against whom he had sinned for his pride. Having recognized this, he raised his eyes to heaven, as if begging for mercy, because the only one who was great & glorious & who had humiliated him & made him the most despicable of all men, was also the only one who could make him the greatest & most respected by all. Therefore God, having received him with mercy, brought him back to his natural sense, & he blessed God by giving Him glory.

As to what he adds, that having blessed & given glory to God & that his form returned does not mean that before he had the shape of an ox, because reason & understanding cannot be lodged within this. Nor should it be understood that this form was either spiritual or corporeal, because he had already mentioned the spiritual, which is the intellectual soul, as well as the corporeal, when he said that he raised his eyes to heaven. Besides, the corporeal cannot remain whole without the spiritual. In this way, therefore, we must understand the external ornament of the human body, which had been depraved & altered by the great abundance of hair that covered the whole body & the excessively sized nails. Now, hair & nails are not parts of the body but only accessories, that is why I have said that this form was not corporeal, but accidental.

For the reasons allegued above, it seems quite clear that Nebuchadnezzar's objection concludes nothing. Nor does that of the Magi of Egypt, whom Bodin recklessly asserts to have actually turned their rods into serpents & frogs. As proof of his assertion, he alleges that, if the serpents of the Magi had been rods, the serpent of Moses would not have digested them, in which he shows himself as if God, who made the rod of Moses into a living & moving serpent, could not also make this serpent devour the rods of the Magicians, which apparently seemed to Pharaoh & the others whose eyes were dazzled & believed, because of the Charmers, to be real serpents.

But God, from whom nothing can be hidden, in order to show that lies cannot last & highlight the truth (which is God himself), allowed the true serpent to devour the false serpents of the Magi, so that glory, power & honor would belong forever to Him. So, sometimes truth fights with falsehood, & for a time truth remains obscured, but in the end it always comes to light, destroying the lie, & remaining victorious.

It is, therefore, an imposture to say that the serpent of Moses could not swallow or digest the rods of the Charmers, as if this serpent, made extraordinarily by the power of God, could not at his will swallow & digest them. For it is no less possible that Moses' serpent swallowed & even digested the Charmer's wands than it is that Moses' rod became a living & moving serpent. But to argue inclusively about the infinite power of God who made everything from nothing, or also discussing or denying the miracles that God works in an extraordinary & supernatural way, in order to confirm his word & make himself formidable among men, is that not impiety & blasphemy?

Thus, Bodin unwisely asserts that the Charmers, with the help of the Devil, have actually transformed the rods into serpents, produced frogs & turned the waters red. In the Holy Bible we are taught the opposite, & especially in the Exodus, where it is said that the Charmers did the same thing through their enchantments. Now, if they did it by enchantment, as is well known, it was not physically but in appearance, placing before the King's eyes the simulated figure of a serpent. Because, as Jamblichus very wisely says in The Book of the Mysteries, "The end of the magical art is not merely to make but only to show in appearance the things that one imagines, of which they have no feet nor head", as we say in common proverb.

This also confirms Saint Clement, when he says that the Egyptian magicians seemed to be making signs instead of actually doing them. For this cause, the pretended serpents of the Charmers were swallowed by the true serpent of Moses, as a sign & revelation of the imposture & evidence of the truth. This is also confirmed by Solomon in *The Book of Wisdom* chapter 17, where, in describing the judgments of God upon the Egyptians who held God's people captive, he says in verse 7, that the illusions of magical art were overthrown with shameful reproach of pride. Likewise, speaking of the terrible punishment of the Egyptians, he says in chapter 18 verse 13, that those who had not believed because of witchcraft confessed to death that the people of Israel were children of God.

Therefore, it seems that all that the Egyptian magicians did was only an illusion & a deception performed with the help of the Demons who moved the convenient moods to receive these illusions, & could fill in the appearances as they saw fit. The visual spirit of the Egyptians who depended on the magicians were idolaters & therefore organs of Satan.

Likewise, the Turks have their own witchcraft with the help of which they forcibly bring back the escaped slaves, after having made imprecations & uttered strange & horrible words. Then, by the power of the Devil, the fugitives thinks that their path is full of dragons & lions, wherever the sea & rivers overflow to come & swallow them, wherever they are in darkness, & these terrors bring them back to their Master.

Returning to our subject, Justin Martyr in the exposition of the questions proposed to the Christians (question number 26), argues that the miracles of the Magi of Egypt were not true miracles, but the works of the Demons that enchanted the eyes of the spectators. But what is there to discuss further, since Saint Paul, even in the second chapter of his second *Epistle to the Thessalonians*, speaks of the destruction & false miracles of the Antichrist.

He says that his presence is in accordance with the operation of Satan, with all power, signs & wonders of falsehood, & with all deception of iniquity in those who perish, & adds to the next verse, that for this cause God will send punishments to those who believe it to be a lie, from which we can easily deduce that many will be seduced by the lying miracles of this son of perdition, & that everything the Magi do is illusory. Here, Saint Augustine also confirms it, when explaining this passage from Saint Paul, where he says that these signs & wonders are called lies, either because they will be seen to be just phantoms or because they will lead men into error.

Let us conclude then, with Saint Augustine, that although the Demons with their great speed can erase & make some things disappear, in their place dragons, serpents or other similar things may appear. We should not think that the matter of these visible things is subject to the will of the transgressive angels, but only to that of God, who reserved the prerogative of creating & transforming creatures into other species. But here it must be taken into account that the Devil cannot always, when he sees fit, create such illusions. In the same way that those whose pure eyes opened by the Eternal cannot be deceived by such illusions, but simply see things as they are, as we read of Hilarion who simply saw & recognized a woman whom the common people he esteemed & believed himself to be a mare.

Furthermore, it should be noted that these illusions are not always created by evil spirits, but also sometimes by good angels, or by God himself, who molded both hearing & vision. This at the request of the faithful, as we read in the second book of *Kings* chapter 3, where it is said that the Moabites, upon learning that Jehoram & Jehoshaphat, kings of Israel, were coming forward to fight against them, gathered together all those who could carry arms, & further up they stopped in their march. The next morning, when the sun had risen over the waters, the Moabites saw the waters red as blood, then they said: "It is blood!" The kings fought among themselves & beat each other. Now the Moabites fled & came to the tents of Israel, so the Israelites arose & defeated the Moabites & destroyed their cities.

In the same book, chapter 6, we also read that, by the prayer of Elisha, God struck the Syrians with blindness, who according to the command of their king had surrounded the city of Dothan by night with a large army, where Elisha stayed. In the same way as also at Elisha's prayer, God opened his eyes to see the heavenly army, by which Elisha found himself surrounded, to protect him from all danger & to secure him against his enemies. In the same book, chapter 7 verse 6, we read that the Lord laid siege to the camp of the Syrians that they had in Samaria when they heard the roar of chariots & horses & a great army, so much so that they said to one another: "Behold, the king of Israel hired the kings of the Ethiopians & the kings of Egypt to come against us, they rose up & fled at dawn, they left their tents, their horses, their donkeys & the camp as it was & fled to save their lives."

Bodin falsely wanted to demonstrate the opposite by perverting the meaning of the sacred story. What Johannes Trithemius Abbot says is that in the year 970 there was a Jew named Bayan, son of Simeon Prince of the Bulgarians, who turned into a wolf & became invisible when he wanted. Now, who is it that, even if he is a little versed in letters, assures that a body composed of four elements can become invisible naturally to our healthy & complete eye in the middle of noon, or at night in the light? If such & such were true, wouldn't it be necessary to confess that the body is reduced to Plato's atoms? & which is then gathered into a body by the competition of the influence of the stars, as Plato teaches, that, if it were, the second form of the body would be different from the first, especially because any individual of whatever species always receives something special at birth to distinguish him from others of his species. But since these atoms are nothing more than strange things & dreams of Plato, or rather chimeras constructed in the air, Bodin's conclusion is also similar.

Therefore, since this invisibility cannot be accomplished, since the nature of composite bodies is repugnant to it, I conclude that it is illusory, as is also the transformation into a wolf. Now, although these things agree that they were both done by the Devil's artifice, they do differ as to their purpose, because one shows us what is not, & the other prevents us from seeing what is. In the first, the imaginative is deceived by the representation of a false & vain figure. In the second, the eyes are dazzled & enchanted, or the Devil prevents the eyes of the audience from looking at the body of Bayan, which he has taken as protection & under his shadow. Just as Bayan's body was made invisible by diabolical illusion, so similarly he was transformed into a wolf illusorily by the same artifice of the Devil, to whom he was a slave.

Thus, the Witch Circe, a very famous ancient Witch, illusorily transformed, as Homer tells us, Ulysses' companions into pigs by means of potions, but this was by illusions. She didn't really transform them into pigs as Bodin maintains. Saint Chrysostom denies it when he says that the sorceress Circe had seduced Ulysses' companions for sensual pleasure in such a way that they were like pigs unto he, thereby demonstrating very clearly that their bodies were not changed, but only that their reason was disturbed & brutalized by their disordered appetites & intemperance. This is also confirmed by Socrates (as Xenophon says at the beginning of the *Sayings & Acts of Socrates*) because after having praised temperance, & given some precept for observing it, he says that he considers that Circe transformed Ulysses' companions into pigs which she fed with various meats & that Ulysses, partly by Minerva's advice, & partly by his abstinence, had secured such brutality.

Thus, the Poets pretended that the Arcades had become wolves, especially because they lived like wolves, since, like cruel & bestial men, they fed on raw flesh & human flesh. Quite rightly, Pliny, mocking such daydreams, says that we must assume that it is something unbelievable to say that men turn into wolves & then return to what they were, or else believe all the things that we believe have happened in the past centuries. The same in book 10, chapter 44, he adds that it is wonderful how the foolish belief of the Greeks spread, because there is no lie so reckless that does not have a witness.

But returning to our author Bodin, let us see whether the arguments he alleges to prove that the Devil can separate the soul from the body of the Sorcerers to return it afterwards, have more force than those he has alleged to sustain the transformation of men into beasts. Let us begin with the metamorphose of Virgil (which he quotes incorrectly on purpose) contained in book 6 of his Aeneid, where he discusses the enchantments of the Witch Circe, so celebrated by the Poets, & says, *Que se carminibus promittat soluere mentes*, that she boasts of being able to enrapture the mind in ecstasy. & this we must be understand as the result of strong & assiduous meditation & contemplation of elevated things, in which the spirit, united & connected, forgets itself, as if it were absent from the body & detached from the senses.

We must not, therefore, understand this ecstasy as a separation of the soul from the body, as Bodin would infer, which is why Virgil mocks him, & merely tells of

Circe's ridiculous boast without stating anything about it. For there is no man who believes that by some means of the Devil one can take the Moon out of the Sky, make the rivers turn towards the mountain with great haste, change mountains into valleys & valleys into mountains, cause the souls of the damned to be brought out of Hell, remove the light from the Sky, make the Stars lose their brightness, & similar things that the Witch aforesaid falsely claims to be able to do. However, she is never able to lure Ulysses to her love, even by all her tricks.

Therefore, it seems increasingly clear that these his boasts were nothing but pure lies & vanity, because the power to do such things resides only in the one Creator, the author of All Good. But as always, one absurd approach is followed by several others. For this reason, Bodin was not satisfied only with having wanted to support this alleged transport of the soul, but went further by adding that in truth, the vegetative, vital & animal soul remains, although the senses, movement & reason are lost. A completely monstrous & childish argument, because who has ever seen an animal without feeling, without animal life & movement?

Since it is feeling & movement that makes the animal, & distinguishes it from the Vegetative, as the intellective soul in men distinguishes it from other animals. As proof of the above, he cites & depraves the History of the Witch, that John Baptist Porta wrote in his book *Natural Magic*, & which we have described extensively above. Because instead of what Baptist Porta said, that everything she answered was false, he, on the contrary, said that the news she told from various countries were verified, in which we can recognize his fidelity in quoting the authors.

As for the second argument which he alleges, while it is well known that no soporific plant can prevent man, even when asleep, from feeling the fire applied to the skin, that the Witches feel no fire nor pain whatsoever while they are happily in ecstasy. To this argument we will answer with distinction, for it is necessary to distinguish the sleep caused only by narcotic medications, from that of the Witches, which is caused by drugs that not only have the virtue of making you sleep very deeply, but also create various images in phantasy, in addition to those that the Devil manifests to them. & this causes the reasoning of these Witches, who are greatly influenced by the Devil's figures & such drugs, to feel much less than the others, who are simply lulled to sleep without having the imagination disturbed by any figure. & the Devil helps them a lot in that regard, since it is very easy for him to deprive them of any feeling for some time, so that his tricks may not be discovered.

So, on several occasions I have seen Witches who, despite the fact that a stone weighing about two hundred pounds had been placed on top of their feet, did not feel pain & did not move either, for the Devil (as many afterwards confessed) had entered into them, which destroyed both their sense & the movement of their tongues. & so, many of them, charmed by the Devil, resist arquebus bullets, the edges & points of swords, without receiving any harm other than a black bruise. From which it appears that Bodin's argument is in all its conclusions false & inept, as it is for the one that he put as a last refuge & to which, he says, no one has yet responded. In order to demonstrate that it is neither ointment nor a dream, but a true ecstasy of the soul out of the body, he says that all those who go out of the body return half an hour later & as soon as they want, & that this is impossible for the ones who fall asleep with mere narcotics. To what I reply that it is no more inconvenient for Satan to dissipate & drive away all these vain figures by awakening the body, than to arouse such representations & numb the senses.

These arguments together with those previously alleged will now be sufficient to refute the erroneous opinion of Bodin, whereupon we shall conclude in accordance with the testimonies given above both from the Holy Bible & from The Fathers (referring to the priests), as well as from ancient theologians & modern ones, an even from Philosophers & Pagans, that it isn't in the power of the Devil nor Witches to transform one body into another, nor to separate the soul from the body for some time, in order to return to it later. & that, (according to the Decrees) whoever thinks that a creature is created or transmuted into better or worse, or transformed into another species or likeness by another than God, is more evil than a heathen or an infidel.

To God then, the only wise, immortal & invisible, be honor & glory forever & ever.

Amen.

END.

We, Doctors of the Faculty of Theology of Paris, certify that we have seen & read this book entitled *On Lycanthropy, Transformation & Ecstasy of Sorcerers* composed by Monsieur Jean de Nynauld, Doctor of Medicine, in whose book we have found nothing that does not conform to the faith & doctrine of the Catholic, Apostolic & Roman Church.

Done in Paris on April 6, 1615.

M. Coliin, Syndic.

Forgemont.

Dei Sanguis Sanguis Lupi
Lupi Sanguis Sanguis Dei
Omnes Spine Dentes Dei
Lupi Dentes Dentes Dei

HEXEN PRESS
MMXXIV